Leaves of Gold

DAILY PLANNER

Plans, Promises and Prayers for Each New Day

Brownlow
PERSONAL REFLECTIONS
Brownlow Publishing Company, Inc.

Daily Planner features:

As practical and beautiful as it is inspirational, you'll find this planner is a delightful gift for friends...or for yourself. It features:

- 52 ample, non-dated spaces for weekly planning entries
- Inspiring quotations from *Leaves of Gold*, the most popular keepsake anthology of all time
- An encouraging Scripture promise for each week, to refresh the spirit
- Trendsetting design with space for personal information, addresses & phone numbers
- Durable spiral binding

DAILY PLANNER
Copyright © 1995
by Brownlow Publishing Company, Inc.
6309 Airport Freeway
Fort Worth, Texas 76117

English Cottage Edition
ISBN: 1-57051-063-6

Tea TIme Edition
ISBN: 1-57051-064-4

All Scripture references taken from the *New International Version* (NIV) and used by permission.

Personal Information

Name _____
Address _____
_____

Home phone # _____
Work phone # _____
Social Security # _____
Driver's License # _____
Health Insurance _____

Car Insurance _____

Health Information _____
_____
_____

In Case of Emergency, Call _____
_____
_____

Other Helpful Information _____
_____
_____
_____
_____
_____
_____
_____

Year at a Glance

JANUARY	FEBRUARY	MARCH

APRIL	MAY	JUNE

JULY	AUGUST	SEPTEMBER

OCTOBER	NOVEMBER	DECEMBER

Year at a Glance 1995

JANUARY 1995
```
                1  2  3  4  5  6  7
 8  9 10 11 12 13 14
15 16 17 18 19 20 21
22 23 24 25 26 27 28
29 30 31
```

FEBRUARY 1995
```
          1  2  3  4
 5  6  7  8  9 10 11
12 13 14 15 16 17 18
19 20 21 22 23 24 25
26 27 28
```

MARCH 1995
```
          1  2  3  4
 5  6  7  8  9 10 11
12 13 14 15 16 17 18
19 20 21 22 23 24 25
26 27 28 29 30 31
```

APRIL 1995
```
                   1
 2  3  4  5  6  7  8
 9 10 11 12 13 14 15
16 17 18 19 20 21 22
23 24 25 26 27 28 29
30
```

MAY 1995
```
    1  2  3  4  5  6
 7  8  9 10 11 12 13
14 15 16 17 18 19 20
21 22 23 24 25 26 27
28 29 30 31
```

JUNE 1995
```
             1  2  3
 4  5  6  7  8  9 10
11 12 13 14 15 16 17
18 19 20 21 22 23 24
25 26 27 28 29 30
```

JULY 1995
```
                   1
 2  3  4  5  6  7  8
 9 10 11 12 13 14 15
16 17 18 19 20 21 22
23 24 25 26 27 28 29
30 31
```

AUGUST 1995
```
       1  2  3  4  5
 6  7  8  9 10 11 12
13 14 15 16 17 18 19
20 21 22 23 24 25 26
27 28 29 30 31
```

SEPTEMBER 1995
```
                1  2
 3  4  5  6  7  8  9
10 11 12 13 14 15 16
17 18 19 20 21 22 23
24 25 26 27 28 29 30
```

OCTOBER 1995
```
 1  2  3  4  5  6  7
 8  9 10 11 12 13 14
15 16 17 18 19 20 21
22 23 24 25 26 27 28
29 30 31
```

NOVEMBER 1995
```
          1  2  3  4
 5  6  7  8  9 10 11
12 13 14 15 16 17 18
19 20 21 22 23 24 25
26 27 28 29 30
```

DECEMBER 1995
```
                1  2
 3  4  5  6  7  8  9
10 11 12 13 14 15 16
17 18 19 20 21 22 23
24 25 26 27 28 29 30
31
```

Year at a Glance 1996

JANUARY 1996
```
          1  2  3  4  5  6
 7  8  9 10 11 12 13
14 15 16 17 18 19 20
21 22 23 24 25 26 27
28 29 30 31
```

FEBRUARY 1996
```
             1  2  3
 4  5  6  7  8  9 10
11 12 13 14 15 16 17
18 19 20 21 22 23 24
25 26 27 28 29
```

MARCH 1996
```
                   1  2
 3  4  5  6  7  8  9
10 11 12 13 14 15 16
17 18 19 20 21 22 23
24 25 26 27 28 29 30
31
```

APRIL 1996
```
    1  2  3  4  5  6
 7  8  9 10 11 12 13
14 15 16 17 18 19 20
21 22 23 24 25 26 27
28 29 30
```

MAY 1996
```
          1  2  3  4
 5  6  7  8  9 10 11
12 13 14 15 16 17 18
19 20 21 22 23 24 25
26 27 28 29 30 31
```

JUNE 1996
```
                      1
 2  3  4  5  6  7  8
 9 10 11 12 13 14 15
16 17 18 19 20 21 22
23 24 25 26 27 28 29
30
```

JULY 1996
```
    1  2  3  4  5  6
 7  8  9 10 11 12 13
14 15 16 17 18 19 20
21 22 23 24 25 26 27
28 29 30 31
```

AUGUST 1996
```
             1  2  3
 4  5  6  7  8  9 10
11 12 13 14 15 16 17
18 19 20 21 22 23 24
25 26 27 28 29 30 31
```

SEPTEMBER 1996
```
 1  2  3  4  5  6  7
 8  9 10 11 12 13 14
15 16 17 18 19 20 21
22 23 24 25 26 27 28
29 30
```

OCTOBER 1996
```
       1  2  3  4  5
 6  7  8  9 10 11 12
13 14 15 16 17 18 19
20 21 22 23 24 25 26
27 28 29 30 31
```

NOVEMBER 1996
```
                1  2
 3  4  5  6  7  8  9
10 11 12 13 14 15 16
17 18 19 20 21 22 23
24 25 26 27 28 29 30
```

DECEMBER 1996
```
 1  2  3  4  5  6  7
 8  9 10 11 12 13 14
15 16 17 18 19 20 21
22 23 24 25 26 27 28
29 30 31
```

Year at a Glance 1997

JANUARY 1997
			1	2	3	4
5	6	7	8	9	10	11
12	13	14	15	16	17	18
19	20	21	22	23	24	25
26	27	28	29	30	31	

FEBRUARY 1997
						1
2	3	4	5	6	7	8
9	10	11	12	13	14	15
16	17	18	19	20	21	22
23	24	25	26	27	28	

MARCH 1997
						1
2	3	4	5	6	7	8
9	10	11	12	13	14	15
16	17	18	19	20	21	22
23	24	25	26	27	28	29
30	31					

APRIL 1997
		1	2	3	4	5
6	7	8	9	10	11	12
13	14	15	16	17	18	19
20	21	22	23	24	25	26
27	28	29	30			

MAY 1997
				1	2	3
4	5	6	7	8	9	10
11	12	13	14	15	16	17
18	19	20	21	22	23	24
25	26	27	28	29	30	31

JUNE 1997
1	2	3	4	5	6	7
8	9	10	11	12	13	14
15	16	17	18	19	20	21
22	23	24	25	26	27	28
29	30					

JULY 1997
		1	2	3	4	5
6	7	8	9	10	11	12
13	14	15	16	17	18	19
20	21	22	23	24	25	26
27	28	29	30	31		

AUGUST 1997
					1	2
3	4	5	6	7	8	9
10	11	12	13	14	15	16
17	18	19	20	21	22	23
24	25	26	27	28	29	30
31						

SEPTEMBER 1997
	1	2	3	4	5	6
7	8	9	10	11	12	13
14	15	16	17	18	19	20
21	22	23	24	25	26	27
28	29	30				

OCTOBER 1997
			1	2	3	4
5	6	7	8	9	10	11
12	13	14	15	16	17	18
19	20	21	22	23	24	25
26	27	28	29	30	31	

NOVEMBER 1997
						1
2	3	4	5	6	7	8
9	10	11	12	13	14	15
16	17	18	19	20	21	22
23	24	25	26	27	28	29
30						

DECEMBER 1997
	1	2	3	4	5	6
7	8	9	10	11	12	13
14	15	16	17	18	19	20
21	22	23	24	25	26	27
28	29	30	31			

Year at a Glance 1998

JANUARY 1998
			1	2	3
4	5	6	7	8	9	10
11	12	13	14	15	16	17
18	19	20	21	22	23	24
25	26	27	28	29	30	31

FEBRUARY 1998
1	2	3	4	5	6	7
8	9	10	11	12	13	14
15	16	17	18	19	20	21
22	23	24	25	26	27	28

MARCH 1998
1	2	3	4	5	6	7
8	9	10	11	12	13	14
15	16	17	18	19	20	21
22	23	24	25	26	27	28
29	30	31

APRIL 1998
			1	2	3	4
5	6	7	8	9	10	11
12	13	14	15	16	17	18
19	20	21	22	23	24	25
26	27	28	29	30

MAY 1998
					1	2
3	4	5	6	7	8	9
10	11	12	13	14	15	16
17	18	19	20	21	22	23
24	25	26	27	28	29	30
31

JUNE 1998
	1	2	3	4	5	6
7	8	9	10	11	12	13
14	15	16	17	18	19	20
21	22	23	24	25	26	27
28	29	30

JULY 1998
			1	2	3	4
5	6	7	8	9	10	11
12	13	14	15	16	17	18
19	20	21	22	23	24	25
26	27	28	29	30	31

AUGUST 1998
						1
2	3	4	5	6	7	8
9	10	11	12	13	14	15
16	17	18	19	20	21	22
23	24	25	26	27	28	29
30	31

SEPTEMBER 1998
		1	2	3	4	5
6	7	8	9	10	11	12
13	14	15	16	17	18	19
20	21	22	23	24	25	26
27	28	29	30

OCTOBER 1998
				1	2	3
4	5	6	7	8	9	10
11	12	13	14	15	16	17
18	19	20	21	22	23	24
25	26	27	28	29	30	31

NOVEMBER 1998
1	2	3	4	5	6	7
8	9	10	11	12	13	14
15	16	17	18	19	20	21
22	23	24	25	26	27	28
29	30

DECEMBER 1998
		1	2	3	4	5
6	7	8	9	10	11	12
13	14	15	16	17	18	19
20	21	22	23	24	25	26
27	28	29	30	31

GOALS FOR THE YEAR

GOALS FOR THE YEAR

Leaves of Gold

Today is your day and mine, the only day we have, the day in which we play our part. What our part may signify in the great whole we may not understand; but we are here to play it, and now is our time.

—David Starr Jordan

PROMISE FOR THE WEEK

...but those who hope in the Lord will renew their strength. They will soar on wings like eagles; they will run and not grow weary, they will walk and not be faint.

Isaiah 40:31

PLANS FOR THE WEEK OF:
_____ TO_____

Priorities for the week _____

Prayer needs for the week _____

SUNDAY _____

MONDAY _____

TUESDAY

WEDNESDAY

THURSDAY

FRIDAY

SATURDAY

Leaves of Gold

Our deeds are seeds of fate, sown here on earth, but bringing forth their harvest in eternity.

Boardman

PROMISE FOR THE WEEK

Dear friends, now we are children of God, and what we will be has not yet been made known. But we know that when he appears, we shall be like him, for we shall see him as he is.

1 John 3:2

PLANS FOR THE WEEK OF:
_____ TO _____

Priorities for the week _____
_____
_____
_____
_____
_____
_____

Prayer needs for the week _____
_____
_____
_____
_____
_____

SUNDAY _____
_____
_____
_____
_____

MONDAY _____
_____
_____
_____
_____

TUESDAY

WEDNESDAY

THURSDAY

FRIDAY

SATURDAY

Leaves of Gold

Hope is like the sun, which, as we journey toward it, casts the shadow of our burden behind us.

PROMISE FOR THE WEEK

What, then, shall we say in response to this? If God is for us, who can be against us?

Romans 8:31

PLANS FOR THE WEEK OF: _____ TO _____

Priorities for the week _____

Prayer needs for the week _____

SUNDAY _____

MONDAY _____

TUESDAY

WEDNESDAY

THURSDAY

FRIDAY

SATURDAY

Leaves of Gold

Our prayer and God's mercy are like two buckets in a well; while one ascends, the other descends.

Hopkins

PROMISE FOR THE WEEK

For we are God's workmanship, created in Christ Jesus to do good works, which God prepared in advance for us to do.

Ephesians 2:10

PLANS FOR THE WEEK OF: _____ TO _____

Priorities for the week _____

_____
_____
_____
_____
_____
_____
_____

Prayer needs for the week _____

_____
_____
_____
_____
_____
_____

SUNDAY_____

_____
_____
_____
_____

MONDAY_____

_____
_____
_____
_____

TUESDAY _____

WEDNESDAY _____

THURSDAY _____

FRIDAY _____

SATURDAY _____

Leaves of Gold

If I can put one touch of rosy sunset into the life of any man or woman, I shall feel that I have worked with God.

George Macdonald

PROMISE FOR THE WEEK

The Lord has done great things for us, and we are filled with joy.

Psalm 126:3

PLANS FOR THE WEEK OF:
_____ TO _____

Priorities for the week _____

_____
_____
_____
_____
_____
_____

Prayer needs for the week _____

_____
_____
_____
_____
_____

SUNDAY _____

_____
_____
_____
_____

MONDAY _____

_____
_____
_____
_____

TUESDAY _____

WEDNESDAY _____

THURSDAY _____

FRIDAY _____

SATURDAY _____

Leaves of Gold

Those who try to do something and fail are infinitely better than those who try to do nothing and succeed.

Lloyd Jones

PROMISE FOR THE WEEK

Then Jesus declared, "I am the bread of life. He who comes to me will never go hungry, and he who believes in me will never be thirsty."

John 6:35

PLANS FOR THE WEEK OF:
_____ TO _____

Priorities for the week _____

Prayer needs for the week _____

SUNDAY _____

MONDAY _____

TUESDAY

WEDNESDAY

THURSDAY

FRIDAY

SATURDAY

Leaves of Gold

Our duty to God is to make of ourselves the most perfect product of divine incarnation that we can become.

Edgar White Burrill

PROMISE FOR THE WEEK

So we fix our eyes not on what is seen, but on what is unseen. For what is seen is temporary, but what is unseen is eternal.

II Corinthians 4:18

PLANS FOR THE WEEK OF:
_____ TO_____

Priorities for the week _____

Prayer needs for the week _____

SUNDAY_____

MONDAY_____

TUESDAY

WEDNESDAY

THURSDAY

FRIDAY

SATURDAY

Leaves of Gold

If you have built castles in the air, your work need not be lost; that is where they should be. Now put the foundations under them.

Thoreau

PROMISE FOR THE WEEK

The grass withers and the flowers fall, but the word of our God stands forever.

Isaiah 40:8

PLANS FOR THE WEEK OF:
_____ TO _____

Priorities for the week _____

Prayer needs for the week _____

SUNDAY _____

MONDAY _____

TUESDAY

WEDNESDAY

THURSDAY

FRIDAY

SATURDAY

Leaves of Gold

I hate to see things done by halves. If it be right, do it boldly; if it be wrong, leave it undone.

Gilpin

PROMISE FOR THE WEEK

The thief comes only to steal and kill and destroy; I have come that they may have life, and have it to the full.

John 10:10

PLANS FOR THE WEEK OF:
_____ TO _____

Priorities for the week _____

Prayer needs for the week _____

SUNDAY _____

MONDAY _____

TUESDAY _____

WEDNESDAY _____

THURSDAY _____

FRIDAY _____

SATURDAY _____

Leaves of Gold

It is impossible for that person to despair who remembers that his Helper is omnipotent.

Jeremy Taylor

PROMISE FOR THE WEEK

*In God I trust;
I will not be
afraid. What
can man
do to me?*

Psalm 56:11

PLANS FOR THE WEEK OF:
_____ TO _____

Priorities for the week _____

Prayer needs for the week _____

SUNDAY _____

MONDAY _____

TUESDAY

WEDNESDAY

THURSDAY

FRIDAY

SATURDAY

Leaves of Gold

I find the doing of the will of God leaves me no time for disputing about His plans.

Macdonald

PROMISE FOR THE WEEK

What is impossible with men is possible with God.

Luke 18:27

PLANS FOR THE WEEK OF:
_____ TO_____

Priorities for the week _____

Prayer needs for the week _____

SUNDAY _____

MONDAY _____

TUESDAY

WEDNESDAY

THURSDAY

FRIDAY

SATURDAY

Leaves of Gold

Happiness is a perfume you cannot pour on others without getting a few drops on yourself.

PROMISE FOR THE WEEK

He tends his flock like a shepherd: He gathers the lambs in his arms and carries them close to his heart; he gently leads those that have young.

Isaiah 40:11

PLANS FOR THE WEEK OF:
_____ TO _____

Priorities for the week _____

Prayer needs for the week _____

SUNDAY _____

MONDAY _____

TUESDAY

WEDNESDAY

THURSDAY

FRIDAY

SATURDAY

Leaves of Gold

Be content with your surroundings but not with yourself till you have made the most of them.

PROMISE FOR THE WEEK

But thanks be to God! He gives us the victory through our Lord Jesus Christ.

1 Corinthians 15:57

PLANS FOR THE WEEK OF:
_____ TO _____

Priorities for the week _____

Prayer needs for the week _____

SUNDAY _____

MONDAY _____

TUESDAY _____

WEDNESDAY _____

THURSDAY _____

FRIDAY _____

SATURDAY _____

Leaves of Gold

The secret of happiness is not in doing what one likes, but in liking what one has to do.

Barrie

Leaves of Gold

Happiness is like manna; it is to be gathered in grains, and enjoyed every day. It will not keep; it cannot be accumulated; nor have we got to go out of ourselves or into remote places to gather it, since it is rained down from Heaven, at our very doors.

—Tryon Edwards

Leaves of Gold

Do not keep the alabaster box of your love and friendship sealed up until your friends are dead. Fill their lives with sweetness. Speak approving, cheering words while their ears can hear them, and while their hearts can be thrilled and made happier.

—George W. Childs

PROMISE FOR THE WEEK

Praise be to the Lord, to God our Savior, who daily bears our burdens.

Psalm 68:19

PLANS FOR THE WEEK OF:
_____ TO _____

Priorities for the week _____

Prayer needs for the week _____

SUNDAY _____

MONDAY _____

TUESDAY

WEDNESDAY

THURSDAY

FRIDAY

SATURDAY

Leaves of Gold

I leave God's secrets to Himself. It is happy for me that God makes me of His court, and not of His council.

Joseph Hall

PROMISE FOR THE WEEK

Neither height nor depth, nor anything else in all creation, will be able to separate us from the love of God that is in Christ Jesus our Lord.

Romans 8:39

PLANS FOR THE WEEK OF _____ TO _____

Priorities for the week _____

Prayer needs for the week _____

SUNDAY _____

MONDAY _____

TUESDAY

WEDNESDAY

THURSDAY

FRIDAY

SATURDAY

Leaves of Gold

Our Lord has written the promise of the resurrection, not in books alone, but in every leaf in springtime.

Martin Luther

PROMISE FOR THE WEEK

I have come into the world as a light, so that no one who believes in me should stay in darkness.

John 12:46

PLANS FOR THE WEEK OF:
_____ TO _____

Priorities for the week _____

Prayer needs for the week _____

SUNDAY _____

MONDAY _____

TUESDAY

WEDNESDAY

THURSDAY

FRIDAY

SATURDAY

Leaves of Gold

We must be prepared for every event of life, for there is nothing that is durable.

Menander

PROMISE FOR THE WEEK

The secret things belong to the Lord our God, but the things revealed belong to us and to our children forever....

Deuteronomy 29:29

PLANS FOR THE WEEK OF:
_____ TO _____

Priorities for the week _____

Prayer needs for the week _____

SUNDAY _____

MONDAY _____

TUESDAY

WEDNESDAY

THURSDAY

FRIDAY

SATURDAY

Leaves of Gold

When God shuts a door He opens a window.

PROMISE FOR THE WEEK

The Lord does not look at the things man looks at. Man looks at the outward appearance, but the Lord looks at the heart.

I Samuel 16:5

PLANS FOR THE WEEK OF: _____ TO _____

Priorities for the week _____

Prayer needs for the week _____

SUNDAY _____

MONDAY _____

TUESDAY

WEDNESDAY

THURSDAY

FRIDAY

SATURDAY

Leaves of Gold

He who can not forgive others breaks the bridge over which he must pass himself.

George Herbert

PROMISE FOR THE WEEK

Weeping may remain for a night, but rejoicing comes in the morning.

Psalm 30:5

PLANS FOR THE WEEK OF:
_____ TO _____

Priorities for the week

Prayer needs for the week

SUNDAY

MONDAY

TUESDAY

WEDNESDAY

THURSDAY

FRIDAY

SATURDAY

Leaves of Gold

By many hands the work of God is done.

Richard Le Gallienne

PROMISE FOR THE WEEK

The Lord himself goes before you and will be with you; he will never leave you nor forsake you. Do not be afraid; do not be discouraged.

Deuteronomy 31:8

PLANS FOR THE WEEK OF:
_____ TO _____

Priorities for the week _____

Prayer needs for the week _____

SUNDAY _____

MONDAY _____

TUESDAY

WEDNESDAY

THURSDAY

FRIDAY

SATURDAY

Leaves of Gold

Never be afraid of giving up your best, and God will give you His better.

Hinton

PROMISE FOR THE WEEK

The earth is full of his unfailing love. Blessed is the nation whose God is the Lord....

Psalm 33:5,12

PLANS FOR THE WEEK OF:
_____ TO _____

Priorities for the week _____

Prayer needs for the week _____

SUNDAY _____

MONDAY _____

TUESDAY

WEDNESDAY

THURSDAY

FRIDAY

SATURDAY

Leaves of Gold

I have lived long enough to thank God that all my prayers have not been answered.

Jean Ingelow

PROMISE FOR THE WEEK

A cheerful heart is good medicine....

Proverbs 17:22

PLANS FOR THE WEEK OF: _____ TO _____

Priorities for the week

Prayer needs for the week

SUNDAY

MONDAY

TUESDAY

WEDNESDAY

THURSDAY

FRIDAY

SATURDAY

Leaves of Gold

Those who run from God in the morning will scarcely find him the rest of the day.

Bunyan

PROMISE FOR THE WEEK

I love the Lord, for he heard my voice; he heard my cry for mercy. Because he turned his ear to me, I will call on him as long as I live.

Psalm 116:1,2

PLANS FOR THE WEEK OF:
_____ TO _____

Priorities for the week

Prayer needs for the week

SUNDAY

MONDAY

TUESDAY _____

WEDNESDAY _____

THURSDAY _____

FRIDAY _____

SATURDAY _____

Leaves of Gold

Joy is not in things; it is in us.

Wagner

PROMISE FOR THE WEEK

I delight greatly in the Lord; my soul rejoices in my God. For he has clothed me with garments of salvation and arrayed me in a robe of righteousness....

Isaiah 61:10

PLANS FOR THE WEEK OF:
_____ TO _____

Priorities for the week _____

_____
_____
_____
_____
_____
_____
_____

Prayer needs for the week _____

_____
_____
_____
_____
_____
_____
_____

SUNDAY _____

_____
_____
_____
_____

MONDAY _____

_____
_____
_____
_____

TUESDAY

WEDNESDAY

THURSDAY

FRIDAY

SATURDAY

Leaves of Gold

I will not follow where the path may lead, but I will go where there is no path, and I will leave a trail.

Muriel Strode

PROMISE FOR THE WEEK

As the mountains surround Jerusalem, so the Lord surrounds his people both now and forever.

Psalm 125:2

PLANS FOR THE WEEK OF:
_____ TO _____

Priorities for the week _____

Prayer needs for the week _____

SUNDAY _____

MONDAY _____

TUESDAY

WEDNESDAY

THURSDAY

FRIDAY

SATURDAY

Leaves of Gold

If religion has done nothing for your temper, it has done nothing for your soul.

Clayton

PROMISE FOR THE WEEK

Your Father knows what you need before you ask him.

Matthew 6:8

PLANS FOR THE WEEK OF:
_____ TO_____

Priorities for the week _____

_____
_____
_____
_____
_____
_____

Prayer needs for the week _____

_____
_____
_____
_____
_____

SUNDAY_____

_____
_____
_____
_____

MONDAY_____

_____
_____
_____
_____

TUESDAY _____

WEDNESDAY _____

THURSDAY _____

FRIDAY _____

SATURDAY _____

Leaves of Gold

It is not sufficient to have great qualities; we must be able to make proper use of them.

La Rochefoucauld

Leaves of Gold

Blessed are they
who have the gift
of making friends,
for it is one of God's
best gifts. It involves
many things, but
above all, the power
of going out of one's
self, and appreciating
whatever is noble and
loving in another.

—Thomas hughes

Leaves of Gold

God brings no
man into the conflicts
of life to desert him.
Every man has a
Friend in Heaven
whose resources
are unlimited; and
on Him he may call
at any hour and
find sympathy
and assistance.

—Morris

PROMISE FOR THE WEEK

...Lord, to whom shall we go? You have the words of eternal life. We believe and know that you are the Holy One of God.

John 6:68,69

PLANS FOR THE WEEK OF:
_____ TO _____

Priorities for the week _____

Prayer needs for the week _____

SUNDAY _____

MONDAY _____

TUESDAY

WEDNESDAY

THURSDAY

FRIDAY

SATURDAY

Leaves of Gold

The true calling of a Christian is not to do extraordinary things, but to do ordinary things in an extraordinary way.

Dean Stanley

PROMISE FOR THE WEEK

And surely I will be with you always, to the very end of the age.

Matthew 28:20

PLANS FOR THE WEEK OF:
_____ TO_____

Priorities for the week _____

_____
_____
_____
_____
_____
_____
_____

Prayer needs for the week _____

_____
_____
_____
_____
_____
_____

SUNDAY _____

_____
_____
_____
_____

MONDAY _____

_____
_____
_____
_____

TUESDAY

WEDNESDAY

THURSDAY

FRIDAY

SATURDAY

Leaves of Gold

Nature is the cloak of God that reveals Him to the wise, and hides Him from the foolish.

Thomas Carlyle

PROMISE FOR THE WEEK

You are my friends if you do what I command.

John 15:14

PLANS FOR THE WEEK OF:
_____ TO _____

Priorities for the week _____

_____
_____
_____
_____
_____
_____

Prayer needs for the week _____

_____
_____
_____
_____
_____

SUNDAY _____

_____
_____
_____
_____

MONDAY _____

_____
_____
_____
_____

TUESDAY

WEDNESDAY

THURSDAY

FRIDAY

SATURDAY

Leaves of Gold

It is not what he has, nor even what he does, which directly expresses the worth of a man, but what he is.

Henri-Frederic Amiel

PROMISE FOR THE WEEK

And we know that in all things God works for the good of those who love him....

Romans 8:28

PLANS FOR THE WEEK OF:
_____ TO _____

Priorities for the week _____

Prayer needs for the week _____

SUNDAY _____

MONDAY _____

TUESDAY

WEDNESDAY

THURSDAY

FRIDAY

SATURDAY

Leaves of Gold

Thank God every morning when you get up that you have something to do which must be done, whether you like it or not.

Charles Kingsley

PROMISE FOR THE WEEK

Though outwardly we are wasting away, yet inwardly we are being renewed day by day.

II Corinthians 4:16

PLANS FOR THE WEEK OF: _____ TO _____

Priorities for the week _____

Prayer needs for the week _____

SUNDAY _____

MONDAY _____

TUESDAY

WEDNESDAY

THURSDAY

FRIDAY

SATURDAY

Leaves of Gold

When love and skill work together expect a masterpiece.

John Ruskin

PROMISE FOR THE WEEK

I have been crucified with Christ and I no longer live, but Christ lives in me.

Galatians 2:20

PLANS FOR THE WEEK OF:
_____ TO _____

Priorities for the week _____

_____
_____
_____
_____
_____
_____

Prayer needs for the week _____

_____
_____
_____
_____
_____

SUNDAY _____

_____
_____
_____
_____

MONDAY _____

_____
_____
_____
_____

TUESDAY _____

WEDNESDAY _____

THURSDAY _____

FRIDAY _____

SATURDAY _____

Leaves of Gold

Just as there comes a warm sunbeam into every cottage window, so comes a love-beam of God's care and pity for every separate need.

Nathaniel Hawthorne

PROMISE FOR THE WEEK

Therefore, if anyone is in Christ, he is a new creation; the old has gone, the new has come!

II Corinthians 5:17

PLANS FOR THE WEEK OF: _____ TO _____

Priorities for the week _____

Prayer needs for the week _____

SUNDAY _____

MONDAY _____

TUESDAY _____

WEDNESDAY _____

THURSDAY _____

FRIDAY _____

SATURDAY _____

Leaves of Gold

Doubt is the vestibule through which all must pass before they can enter the temple of wisdom.

Colton

PROMISE FOR THE WEEK

And my God will meet all your needs according to his glorious riches in Christ Jesus.

Philippians 4:19

PLANS FOR THE WEEK OF:
_____ TO _____

Priorities for the week _____

Prayer needs for the week _____

SUNDAY _____

MONDAY _____

TUESDAY

WEDNESDAY

THURSDAY

FRIDAY

SATURDAY

Leaves of Gold

Tears are often the telescope through which men see far into heaven.

Henry Ward Beecher

PROMISE FOR THE WEEK

Come near to God and he will come near to you....

James 4:8

PLANS FOR THE WEEK OF:
_____ TO _____

Priorities for the week _____

Prayer needs for the week _____

SUNDAY _____

MONDAY _____

TUESDAY

WEDNESDAY

THURSDAY

FRIDAY

SATURDAY

Leaves of Gold

There is a wealth of unexpressed love in the world.

Arthur Hopkins

PROMISE FOR THE WEEK

...I will put my laws in their hearts, and I will write them on their minds.... Their sins and lawless acts I will remember no more.

Hebrews 10:16,17

PLANS FOR THE WEEK OF:
_____ TO _____

Priorities for the week _____

Prayer needs for the week _____

SUNDAY _____

MONDAY _____

TUESDAY

WEDNESDAY

THURSDAY

FRIDAY

SATURDAY

Leaves of Gold

Be not afraid in misfortune. When God causes a tree to be hewn down He takes care that His birds can nestle on another.

PROMISE FOR THE WEEK

If any of you lacks wisdom, he should ask God, who gives generously to all without finding fault, and it will be given to him. But when he asks, he must believe and not doubt....

James 1:5,6

PLANS FOR THE WEEK OF:
_____ TO_____

Priorities for the week _____

Prayer needs for the week _____

SUNDAY_____

MONDAY_____

TUESDAY

WEDNESDAY

THURSDAY

FRIDAY

SATURDAY

Leaves of Gold

Fear not that thy life shall come to an end, but rather fear that it shall never have a beginning.

J.H. Newman

PROMISE FOR THE WEEK

How great is the love the Father has lavished on us, that we should be called children of God!...

I John 3:1

PLANS FOR THE WEEK OF:
_____ TO _____

Priorities for the week _____

_____
_____
_____
_____
_____
_____

Prayer needs for the week _____

_____
_____
_____
_____
_____

SUNDAY _____

_____
_____
_____
_____

MONDAY _____

_____
_____
_____
_____

TUESDAY

WEDNESDAY

THURSDAY

FRIDAY

SATURDAY

Leaves of Gold

Those who are afraid of the deep will not catch many fish. Have the courage to "launch out."

PROMISE FOR THE WEEK

...The prayer of a righteous man is powerful and effective.

James 5:16

PLANS FOR THE WEEK OF:
_____ TO _____

Priorities for the week _____

_____
_____
_____
_____
_____
_____

Prayer needs for the week _____

_____
_____
_____
_____
_____

SUNDAY _____

_____
_____
_____
_____

MONDAY _____

_____
_____
_____
_____

TUESDAY

WEDNESDAY

THURSDAY

FRIDAY

SATURDAY

Leaves of Gold

So long as we love, we serve. So long as we are loved by others I would almost say we are indispensable; and no man is useless while he has a friend.

R.L. Stevenson

Leaves of Gold

Friendship, indeed, is one of the greatest boons God can bestow on man. It is a union of our finest feelings; a disinterested binding of hearts, and a sympathy between two souls. It is an indefinable trust we repose in one another, a constant communication between two minds, and an unremitting anxiety for each other's souls.

—J. Hill

Leaves of Gold

God has a purpose for my life. No other person can take my place. It isn't a big place, to be sure, but for years I have been molded in a peculiar way to fill a peculiar niche in the world's work.

—Charles Stelzle

PROMISE FOR THE WEEK

I write these things to you who believe in the name of the Son of God so that you may know that you have eternal life.

1 John 5:13

PLANS FOR THE WEEK OF
_____ TO _____

Priorities for the week _____

_____
_____
_____
_____
_____
_____

Prayer needs for the week _____

_____
_____
_____
_____
_____

SUNDAY_____

_____
_____
_____
_____

MONDAY_____

_____
_____
_____
_____

TUESDAY

WEDNESDAY

THURSDAY

FRIDAY

SATURDAY

Leaves of Gold

Every house where love abides and friendship is a guest, is surely home, and home, sweet home, for there the heart can rest.

Henry Van Dyke

PROMISE FOR THE WEEK

Blessed are the dead who die in the Lord from now on...they will rest from their labor, for their deeds will follow them.

Revelation 14:13

PLANS FOR THE WEEK OF
_____ TO_____

Priorities for the week _____
_____
_____
_____
_____
_____
_____
_____

Prayer needs for the week _____
_____
_____
_____
_____
_____
_____

SUNDAY_____
_____
_____
_____
_____

MONDAY_____
_____
_____
_____
_____

TUESDAY _____

WEDNESDAY _____

THURSDAY _____

FRIDAY _____

SATURDAY _____

Leaves of Gold

I want it said of me by those who knew me best, that I always plucked a thistle and planted a flower where I thought a flower would grow.

Abraham Lincoln

PROMISE FOR THE WEEK

But if we walk in the light, as he is in the light, we have fellowship with one another, and the blood of Jesus, his Son, purifies us from every sin.

I John 1:7

PLANS FOR THE WEEK OF:
_____ TO_____

Priorities for the week _____
_____
_____
_____
_____
_____
_____
_____

Prayer needs for the week _____
_____
_____
_____
_____
_____
_____

SUNDAY_____
_____
_____
_____
_____

MONDAY_____
_____
_____
_____
_____

TUESDAY

WEDNESDAY

THURSDAY

FRIDAY

SATURDAY

Leaves of Gold

The world is a looking-glass, and gives back to every man the reflection of his own face.

William Makepeace Thackeray

PROMISE FOR THE WEEK

May the God of hope fill you with all joy and peace as you trust in him, so that you may overflow with hope by the power of the Holy Spirit.

Romans 15:13

PLANS FOR THE WEEK OF:
_____ TO_____

Priorities for the week _____

Prayer needs for the week _____

SUNDAY _____

MONDAY _____

TUESDAY _____

WEDNESDAY _____

THURSDAY _____

FRIDAY _____

SATURDAY _____

Leaves of Gold

The mountains are God's thoughts piled up. The ocean is God's thoughts spread out. The flowers are God's thoughts in bloom. The dew drops are God's thoughts in pearls.

Sam Jones

PROMISE FOR THE WEEK

Come to me, all you who are weary and burdened, and I will give you rest.

Matthew 11:28

PLANS FOR THE WEEK OF:
_____ TO _____

Priorities for the week _____

Prayer needs for the week _____

SUNDAY _____

MONDAY _____

TUESDAY

WEDNESDAY

THURSDAY

FRIDAY

SATURDAY

Leaves of Gold

The highest life and glory of man is to be alive unto God.

G.B. Cheever

PROMISE FOR THE WEEK

Then my enemies will turn back when I call for help. By this I will know that God is for me.

Psalm 56:9

PLANS FOR THE WEEK OF:
_____ TO _____

Priorities for the week _____

_____
_____
_____
_____
_____
_____

Prayer needs for the week _____

_____
_____
_____
_____
_____

SUNDAY _____

_____
_____
_____
_____

MONDAY _____

_____
_____
_____
_____

TUESDAY _____

WEDNESDAY _____

THURSDAY _____

FRIDAY _____

SATURDAY _____

Leaves of Gold

There is no happiness in having and getting, but only in giving. Half the world is on the wrong scent in the pursuit of happiness.

F.W. Gunsaulus

PROMISE FOR THE WEEK

I will give them a heart to know me, that I am the Lord. They will be my people, and I will be their God, for they will return to me with all their heart....

Jeremiah 24:7

PLANS FOR THE WEEK OF:
_____ TO _____

Priorities for the week _____

Prayer needs for the week _____

SUNDAY _____

MONDAY _____

TUESDAY _____

WEDNESDAY _____

THURSDAY _____

FRIDAY _____

SATURDAY _____

Leaves of Gold

What I spent I lost; what I possessed is left to others; what I gave away remains with me.

Joseph Addison

PROMISE FOR THE WEEK

Do not be afraid, little flock, for your Father has been pleased to give you the kingdom.

Luke 12:32

PLANS FOR THE WEEK OF:
_____ TO _____

Priorities for the week _____
_____
_____
_____
_____
_____
_____

Prayer needs for the week _____
_____
_____
_____
_____
_____

SUNDAY _____
_____
_____
_____

MONDAY _____
_____
_____
_____

TUESDAY

WEDNESDAY

THURSDAY

FRIDAY

SATURDAY

Leaves of Gold

A prayer in its simplest definition is merely a wish turned God-ward.

Phillips Brooks

PROMISE FOR THE WEEK

The Word became flesh and lived for a while among us. We have seen his glory, the glory of the one and only Son, who came from the Father, full of grace and truth....

John 1:14

PLANS FOR THE WEEK OF:
_____ TO _____

Priorities for the week _____

Prayer needs for the week _____

SUNDAY _____

MONDAY _____

TUESDAY

WEDNESDAY

THURSDAY

FRIDAY

SATURDAY

Leaves of Gold

Great works are performed not by strength, but by perseverance.

PROMISE FOR THE WEEK

I consider that our present sufferings are not worth comparing with the glory that will be revealed in us.

Romans 8:18

PLANS FOR THE WEEK OF:
_____ TO _____

Priorities for the week _____

Prayer needs for the week _____

SUNDAY _____

MONDAY _____

TUESDAY

WEDNESDAY

THURSDAY

FRIDAY

SATURDAY

Leaves of Gold

Live for something. Write your name in kindness, love, and mercy on the hearts of thousands you come in contact with year by year; you will never be forgotten.

Chalmers

PROMISE FOR THE WEEK

All Scripture is God-breathed and is useful for teaching, rebuking, correcting and training in righteousness, so that the man of God may be thoroughly equipped for every good work.

II Timothy 3:16, 17

PLANS FOR THE WEEK OF:
_____ TO_____

Priorities for the week _____

Prayer needs for the week _____

SUNDAY_____

MONDAY_____

TUESDAY _____

WEDNESDAY _____

THURSDAY _____

FRIDAY _____

SATURDAY _____

Leaves of Gold

God has given us tongues that we may say something pleasant to our fellow-men.

Heinrich Heine

PROMISE FOR THE WEEK

Let us then approach the throne of grace with confidence, so that we may receive mercy and find grace to help us in our time of need.

Hebrews 4:16

PLANS FOR THE WEEK OF:
_____ TO _____

Priorities for the week _____

Prayer needs for the week _____

SUNDAY _____

MONDAY _____

TUESDAY

WEDNESDAY

THURSDAY

FRIDAY

SATURDAY

Leaves of Gold

How sweet the words of truth breathed from the lips of love.

James Beattie

PROMISE FOR THE WEEK

...But if anybody does sin, we have one who speaks to the Father in our defense—Jesus Christ, the Righteous One.

1 John 2:1

PLANS FOR THE WEEK OF:
_____ TO _____

Priorities for the week

Prayer needs for the week

SUNDAY

MONDAY

TUESDAY _____

WEDNESDAY _____

THURSDAY _____

FRIDAY _____

SATURDAY _____

Leaves of Gold

If it wasn't for the optimist, the pessimist would never know how happy he wasn't.

Leaves of Gold

It's good to have money and the things that money can buy, but it's good, too, to check up once in a while and make sure you haven't lost the things that money can't buy

—George Horace Lorimer

Leaves of Gold

I love you not only for what you are, but for what I am when I am with you. I love you not only for what you have made of yourself, but for what you are making of me. I love you for the part of me that you bring out.

Addresses & Phone Numbers

Name	Name
Address	Address
Home Phone	Home Phone
Work Phone	Work Phone
Name	Name
Address	Address
Home Phone	Home Phone
Work Phone	Work Phone
Name	Name
Address	Address
Home Phone	Home Phone
Work Phone	Work Phone
Name	Name
Address	Address
Home Phone	Home Phone
Work Phone	Work Phone

Addresses & Phone Numbers

Name	Name
Address	Address
Home Phone	Home Phone
Work Phone	Work Phone
Name	Name
Address	Address
Home Phone	Home Phone
Work Phone	Work Phone
Name	Name
Address	Address
Home Phone	Home Phone
Work Phone	Work Phone
Name	Name
Address	Address
Home Phone	Home Phone
Work Phone	Work Phone

Addresses & Phone Numbers

Name	Name
Address	Address
Home Phone	Home Phone
Work Phone	Work Phone
Name	Name
Address	Address
Home Phone	Home Phone
Work Phone	Work Phone
Name	Name
Address	Address
Home Phone	Home Phone
Work Phone	Work Phone
Name	Name
Address	Address
Home Phone	Home Phone
Work Phone	Work Phone

Addresses & Phone Numbers

Name	Name
Address	Address
Home Phone	Home Phone
Work Phone	Work Phone
Name	Name
Address	Address
Home Phone	Home Phone
Work Phone	Work Phone
Name	Name
Address	Address
Home Phone	Home Phone
Work Phone	Work Phone
Name	Name
Address	Address
Home Phone	Home Phone
Work Phone	Work Phone

handwritten notes:
- call to block
- 885-7614
- 943-0814
- 954-6222
- phone number

Leaves of Gold

All the quotations in this planner except Scripture references, are taken from *Leaves of Gold*, America's favorite keepsake album of inspirational prose and poetry. For many families, it is a time-honored tradition that continues to delight and inspire all who read it.

If you would like a complete volume of *Leaves of Gold*, for yourself and special friends, it is available at fine bookstores everywhere.